CW00864101

JOE
BIDEN

Rachael L. Thomas

Checkerboard
Library

An Imprint of Abdo Publishing
abdobooks.com

ABDOBOOKS.COM

Printed in the United States of America, North Mankato, Minnesota
102020
012021

THIS BOOK CONTAINS RECYCLED MATERIALS

Design: Emily O'Malley, Kelly Doudna, Mighty Media, Inc.
Production: Mighty Media, Inc.
Editor: Liz Salzmann
Cover Photograph: Matt Rourke/AP/Shutterstock Images
Interior Photographs: Albert de Bruijn/iStockphoto, p. 37; Andrew Harnik/AP Images, p. 33; AP Images, pp. 6, 15, 17, 36; Carolyn Kaster/AP Images, pp. 7 (top right), 25, 29; David Lienemann/Wikimedia Commons, p. 5; Denis Paquin/AP Images, pp. 7 (top left), 21; Everett Collection NYC, pp. 7, 23; Library of Congress, p. 40; Paul Sancya/AP Images, p. 27; Pete Souza/Flickr, p. 44; Shutterstock Images, pp. 18, 31, 38, 39; Wikimedia Commons, pp. 5 (signature), 6 (top left), 11, 12, 13, 40 (Washington), 42

Library of Congress Control Number: 2020948560

Publisher's Cataloging-in-Publication Data
Names: Thomas, Rachael L., author.
Title: Joe Biden / by Rachael L. Thomas
Description: Minneapolis, Minnesota : Abdo Publishing, 2021 | Series: The United States presidents | Includes online resources and index.
Identifiers: ISBN 9781532193811 (lib. bdg.) | ISBN 9781644945261 (pbk.) | ISBN 9781098212452 (ebook)
Subjects: LCSH: Biden, Joseph R., Jr.--Juvenile literature. | Presidents--Juvenile literature. | Presidents--United States--History--Juvenile literature. | Legislators--United States--Biography--Juvenile literature. | Politics and government--Biography--Juvenile literature.
Classification: DDC 973.93--dc23

★ CONTENTS ★

Joe Biden 4

Timeline 6

Did You Know? 9

Joey Biden 10

Education and Marriage 12

Councilman Biden 14

Family Tragedy 16

A Second Chance at Life 18

Senator Biden 20

Election 2008 22

Vice Presidential Duties 24

Charitable Causes 26

The Final Campaign 28

President Biden 32

Office of the President 34

Presidents and Their Terms 40

Glossary 46

Online Resources 47

Index 48

Joe Biden

In November 2020, Joseph Robinette Biden Jr. was elected the forty-sixth president of the United States. By the time of the election, Biden had worked in government for 50 years. At 77 years old, he was the oldest person ever elected US president.

During his career, Biden first trained as a lawyer. In later years, he was elected to the US Senate. As Senator, Biden became an expert in foreign policy. He was also tough on crime.

In 2008, Biden was elected vice president when Barack Obama was elected president. As vice president, Biden advised President Obama on important matters, such as the wars in Iraq and Afghanistan.

Biden's long experience in office later helped his 2020 presidential campaign. People trusted in his experience as a leader. Biden promised progress in healthcare and **environmental** law. As president, Biden led the country during a time of great economic and social turmoil.

★ TIMELINE ★

1942

On November 20, Joseph Robinette Biden Jr. was born in Scranton, Pennsylvania.

1968

Biden graduated from the University of Syracuse with a law degree. The Biden family moved to Wilmington, Delaware.

1973

On January 5, Biden was sworn in as Senator from his sons' hospital room in Wilmington.

1970

Biden started his political career by winning a seat on the New Castle County Council.

1988

Biden underwent three surgeries for brain aneurysms and a blood clot in his lungs.

1972

On November 7, the citizens of Delaware elected Biden to the US Senate.

1961

Biden began attending the University of Delaware. He studied history and political science.

1994

Biden supported the Violent Crime Control and Law Enforcement Act and the Violence Against Women Act (VAWA).

2017

Obama presented Biden with the Presidential Medal of Freedom.

August 2020

Biden announced Senator Kamala Harris as his running mate in the presidential race.

2012

Obama and Biden were re-elected to office.

2019

On April 25, Biden officially launched his 2020 presidential campaign.

November 2020

Biden was elected the forty-sixth president of the United States.

2010

Biden helped secure the New START nuclear arms treaty.

2008

In November, Barack Obama won the presidential election with Biden as his running mate.

" Our future cannot depend on the government alone. **The ultimate solutions lie in the attitudes and the actions** of the American people."

JOE BIDEN

DID YOU KNOW?

★ Those serving in the US Senate must be at least 30 years old. Biden first won the Senate election at age 29. He turned 30 about six weeks before officially taking office.

★ Biden was the longest-serving Delaware senator in history. He was re-elected to the position six times, serving for a total of 36 years.

★ As the 47th vice president of the United States, Biden traveled more than 1.2 million miles (1.9 million km) to more than 50 countries.

★ Biden selecting Senator Kamala Harris as his running mate made US history. She was the first woman of color to ever be elected as vice president.

Joey Biden

Joseph Robinette Biden Jr. was born on November 20, 1942, in Scranton, Pennsylvania. He was the oldest of four children. His family called him Joey.

Joey's mother was Catherine Eugenia Finnegan. She looked after Joey and his brothers and sister. Joey's father was Joseph Robinette Biden Sr. Joseph cleaned boilers for a heating company.

As a child, Joey had a stutter. For example, when he said his last name, he often repeated the first **syllable**. This led his classmates to call him "Bye-Bye." To overcome his stutter, Joey memorized long poems. Then, he repeated the poems to himself in front of a mirror.

When Joey was ten years old, his father found a job selling cars in Wilmington, Delaware. So, the family moved to Delaware. Joey ended up living most of his life there.

FAST FACTS

BORN: November 20, 1942

WIVES: Neilia Hunter (1942–1972), Jill Tracy Jacobs (1951–)

CHILDREN: 4

POLITICAL PARTY: Democrat

AGE AT INAUGURATION: 78

YEARS SERVED: 2021–

VICE PRESIDENT: Kamala Harris

Joey at ten years old

Education and Marriage

Biden went to high school at Archmere Academy in Delaware. This was a prestigious Catholic **preparatory school**. Biden had dreamed of studying there for a long time. But students had to pay a high **tuition** to attend Archmere. His family could not afford this. So, Biden got a job washing the school's windows and helping take care of the school grounds. The money he earned helped his family pay the tuition.

—— Biden (*second from left*) with fellow students at Archmere ——

At Archmere, Biden was elected class president. He also played wide receiver and halfback on the school football team. In 1960, the team was undefeated. That season, Biden caught 19 touchdown passes.

In 1961, Biden graduated high school and began college at the University of Delaware. There, he studied history and **political science**. It was during these years that Biden began developing a lifelong interest in politics. In his third year at the university, he also met Neilia Hunter. The two began dating.

After graduating from the University of Delaware in 1965, Biden started law school at Syracuse University in Syracuse, New York. The next year, he and Neilia married. After Biden graduated from law school in 1968, the family moved to Wilmington. There, Biden worked at a law firm. He also became more interested in politics.

St. Norbert Hall is Archmere's main classroom building.

Councilman Biden

In Wilmington, Biden and Neilia's family began to grow. Their first son, Joseph R. Biden III, was born in 1969. The family called him Beau. A second boy, Robert Hunter Biden, was born in 1970. A year later, the couple had a daughter, Naomi.

During this time, Biden became a member of the **Democratic** Party. In 1970, he ran for a seat on the New Castle County Council in Delaware. In his campaign, he promised to support building public housing. Biden won the seat. It was his first political position.

Biden served as councilman for two years. Then, at age 29, he ran for a Delaware seat in the US Senate. At the time, the seat was held by **Republican** James Caleb Boggs. Boggs was a very popular Senator. Biden was the only politician who dared to fight Boggs for the seat!

Very few people believed that Biden could win the Senate election. He had little money to pay for his campaign. Most of Biden's campaign staff were family members, including his parents. His sister, Valerie, managed the campaign. But over the summer of 1972,

Biden and Neilia with their sons
at a campaign event in 1972

Biden took the time to speak to voters face-to-face. He spoke of his support for the **environment** and **civil rights**. He also openly opposed the **Vietnam War**, which was unpopular with many Americans.

Biden's ideas, youth, and energy won over the citizens of Delaware. The race was close, but on November 7, Biden was announced the winner. He was the fifth-youngest person ever elected to the US Senate.

Family Tragedy

Just a few weeks after Biden's Senate victory, tragedy struck his family. On December 18, 1972, Biden's wife and three children went to buy a Christmas tree. On their way home, a truck hit their car, causing a serious traffic accident. Biden's two sons were badly hurt in the accident. His wife and daughter were killed.

Biden was heartbroken by the loss of Neilia and Naomi. He considered delaying his political career while he and his sons mourned. But in the end, Biden decided to honor his commitment to the people of Delaware by serving in the Senate.

Biden was sworn in on January 5, 1973. Usually, new Senators are sworn in during a ceremony at the US Capitol Building in Washington, DC. But Biden was allowed to take the oath of office at the Wilmington hospital where his sons were being treated for their injuries. There, he was officially sworn in as a US Senator.

Senators usually live part of the year in Washington, DC. There, they can be close to the US Capitol Building, where the Senate meets. But Biden decided to live full-time in

Wilmington. This would allow him to spend more time with his sons as they recovered.

However, living in Wilmington also meant that Biden had to travel to Washington, DC, to do his job. Biden took the train to and from Washington, DC, every workday. The trip took up to 1 hour and 30 minutes each way. Biden continued to commute by train for the rest of his time in the Senate.

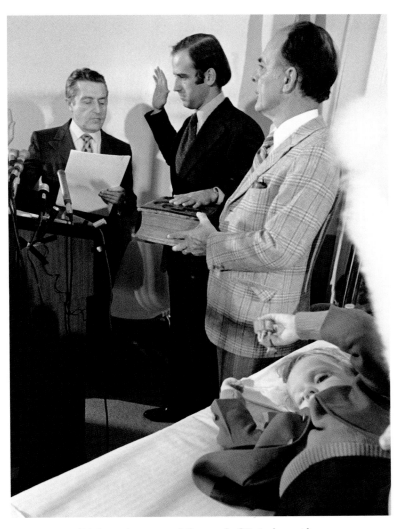

Biden (*second from left*) takes the oath of office beside Beau's hospital bed. Biden's father-in-law, Robert Hunter, holds the Bible for him.

A Second Chance at Life

The years following the death of his wife and daughter were some of the most difficult in Biden's life. He tried to remain strong for his sons. And together, the family began to heal.

Biden with his wife, Jill, on June 9, 1987, after announcing he would run for president in the 1988 election

In 1975, Biden met educator Jill Tracy Jacobs. Two years later, they got married. The couple had a daughter, Ashley, in 1981. In the meantime, Biden's Senate career was going well. By the mid-1980s, Biden was emerging as one of the country's most impressive **Democratic** legislators.

Biden decided to run for president in 1988. He dropped out of the race after he was accused of giving a speech that was partly copied from someone else. However, Biden's health soon became a more serious problem.

During the campaign, Biden had complained of painful headaches. After dropping out of the race, he saw several doctors to find out why he was getting these headaches. The doctors discovered that Biden had two brain **aneurysms**.

In February 1988, Biden underwent brain surgery to remove one of the aneurysms. Three months later, doctors operated on the second aneurysm. Then, Biden required a third surgery for blood clots in his lungs.

Overall, Biden's recovery took seven months. He returned to work at the Senate in September 1988. Biden described his recovery as a "second chance at life" and felt grateful for his family and his work. He vowed to fulfill his role as Senator to the best of his ability.

Senator Biden

Over his time in the Senate, Biden became respected for his knowledge of foreign policy and criminal justice. In 1987, he began serving as Chairman of the Senate Committee on the **Judiciary**. As chairman, Biden helped write the Violent Crime Control and Law Enforcement Act of 1994. The act added 100,000 police officers in cities around the country. It also banned assault weapons and increased prison sentences for several crimes.

Included in the Violent Crime Control and Law Enforcement Act was the Violence Against Women Act (VAWA). The VAWA protected and supported women who had experienced **domestic violence**. This law was an important step in reducing violence against women in the United States.

Over the 1990s, Biden became involved in important foreign policy matters. He worked to end a war in the Balkan **Peninsula** in southeastern Europe. Biden also helped expand the North Atlantic Treaty Organization (NATO) to include several smaller nations that had been part of the Soviet Union.

After almost 30 years in office, Biden was appointed Chairman of the Senate Foreign Relations Committee in 2001. He served in this role twice between 2001 and 2009, for a total of four years. But he had not given up on his dream of becoming president of the United States.

President Bill Clinton signed the Violent Crime Control and Law Enforcement Act on September 13, 1994.

Election 2008

Twenty years after Biden's first run for president, he entered the 2008 presidential race. That year, Biden's presidential run failed to attract much attention. Popular candidates such as Hillary Clinton and Barack Obama received many more votes in **primary** polls. So, Biden again dropped out of the race.

Obama went on to win the **Democratic** primary election in early June. The next question was whom he would choose as his **running mate**. Obama admired Biden's experience and working-class roots. So, he asked Biden to run for vice president and Biden accepted. On August 23, Obama announced that Biden would be his running mate, and the Obama–Biden campaign began.

Obama and Biden worked well together. They communicated a message of economic recovery to the American people. In November 2008, Obama and Biden won the general election. Their **Republican** opponents were John McCain and his running mate, Sarah Palin. On January 20, 2009, Obama and Biden were sworn in as president and vice president of the United States.

On November 4, 2008, (*left to right*) Barack Obama, Michelle Obama, Jill Biden, and Joe Biden celebrated their victory in the 2008 election.

Vice Presidential Duties

As vice president, Biden took an active role advising President Obama. At the time, the United States was fighting wars in Iraq and Afghanistan. Biden helped Obama make decisions about the country's involvement in these wars.

In 2010, Biden worked to secure the New START nuclear arms treaty. This treaty limited the number of nuclear weapons that US and Russian forces could produce and maintain. The treaty improved US security and relations with the Russian Federation.

In 2012, Obama and Biden were re-elected. Later that year, Biden played a leading role **negotiating** a new economic bill. The bill introduced tax increases and spending cuts. These measures helped stop an economic crisis in the country. To pass the bill, Biden needed support from both **Republican** and **Democratic** senators. Biden worked with Republican Mitch McConnell to make the terms of the bill acceptable to both parties.

On the task force, Biden (*center*) worked with many law enforcement experts. These included President of the National Association of Police Organizations Thomas Nee (*left*) and President of the Major Cities Chiefs Association Charles Ramsey (*right*).

Biden also became an important voice on gun control. On December 14, 2012, a mass shooting occurred at Sandy Hook Elementary School in Connecticut. Twenty first graders and six staff members were killed. After the shooting, Biden led a special task force addressing the tragedy. In January 2013, he presented to Obama 27 suggestions to reduce gun violence in the United States. Obama put many of Biden's ideas into action.

Charitable Causes

After two terms in office, Obama stepped down as president on January 20, 2017. Biden's time as vice president also came to an end. Before leaving office, however, Obama presented Biden with the Presidential Medal of Freedom to thank Biden for his service.

For the next few years, Biden concentrated his energy on charitable causes. In February 2017, he and Jill launched the Biden Foundation. This organization aims to continue causes that Biden had worked on as vice president. These include helping more people afford college and preventing violence against women. The following month, Biden also launched the Biden **Cancer** Initiative. This nonprofit organization supports cancer research.

Biden and his wife enjoyed their charitable work. But operations at the Biden Foundation and the Biden Cancer Initiative officially paused in 2019. Biden had a new goal that would require all his time and energy. He was going to run for president in the 2020 election. His opponent would be current **Republican** president Donald Trump.

Biden (*right*) with Beau in 2008. Beau died of brain cancer in 2015. In Beau's honor, his wife, Hallie, started the Beau Biden Foundation for the Protection of Children. This foundation works to end child abuse.

The Final Campaign

On April 25, 2019, Biden released a short video announcing the launch of his 2020 presidential run. In the video, Biden made no mention of policy or laws. Instead, he praised American ideals and values, calling the upcoming election "a battle for the soul of the nation."

Although his campaign got off to a slow start, he eventually became a strong candidate. Millions of people across the country recognized and liked Biden from his time as vice president. He was also seen as a stable and mature leader.

Biden faced strong competition from popular **Democratic** candidates such as Bernie Sanders and Elizabeth Warren. But Biden did better than these candidates in most polls and **primary** elections around the country. Eventually, the other Democratic candidates dropped out of the race.

In the meantime, the **Democratic National Convention** was set to begin on August 17. Six days before the convention, Biden announced that Kamala Harris would be his **running mate**. Harris had worked for many years as a

Harris is African American and Asian American.
She is the first person of color to run for US
vice president as a Democrat or Republican.

lawyer and senator in California. If Biden won the election, she would become the first female vice president of the United States.

During the convention, Biden was officially nominated as the **Democratic** candidate for president. In preparing to continue his campaign, he faced many challenges. The United States was facing two national crises.

Eight months earlier, in December 2019, a dangerous new virus had been discovered in Wuhan, China. The virus caused an illness called COVID-19. COVID-19 soon spread across the world. At the beginning of March 2020, the United States had recorded about 90 cases of COVID-19. By the end of the month, there were more than 180,000 cases.

Over the following months, US cases continued to increase. Most of the nation was placed under lockdown as the virus spread. Shops and other businesses closed. Unemployment rose to levels not seen in almost 100 years.

The country was also facing increased violence and racial **discrimination**. In May 2020, George Floyd died in an encounter with police in Minneapolis, Minnesota. Floyd was one of many African Americans who had been killed during interactions with police in the United States over the past several years.

People in Minneapolis and other cities held protests after Floyd's death. The protesters called for an end to **racism** and violence against African Americans, especially by police officers. Some of the protests turned into **riots**. Many stores and other buildings were robbed and burned. Whoever won the 2020 election would lead a country suffering from the effects of major social and economic problems.

People gather in Minneapolis to demand justice for Floyd and other African Americans killed by police. Many protesters wear face masks to protect themselves and others from COVID-19.

President Biden

Because of the COVID-19 **pandemic**, Biden conducted most of his campaign remotely. He gave interviews and spoke about his views on issues such as climate change, **racism**, and healthcare on video. Typical campaign events such as rallies and door-to-door visits were cancelled.

Election Day was November 3, 2020. That day, about 60 million people went to the polls to vote. However, many people worried that COVID-19 would spread at crowded voting locations. So, they voted early or by mail. More than 100 million people voted this way.

About 65 percent of eligible Americans voted in the 2020 presidential election. This was the highest percentage since 1908. It took four days to determine the outcome. On November 7, Biden and Harris were declared the winners.

That evening, Biden addressed the nation. In his speech, he vowed to help the nation heal from its current crises. He said, "I pledge to be a president who seeks not to divide but unify." His time in office was defined by this promise.

Biden gave his November 7th speech outside a convention center in Wilmington. People watched and listened from their cars in the parking lot.

BRANCHES OF GOVERNMENT

The US government is divided into three branches. They are the executive, legislative, and judicial branches. This division is called a separation of powers. Each branch has some power over the others. This is called a system of checks and balances.

★ EXECUTIVE BRANCH

The executive branch enforces laws. It is made up of the president, the vice president, and the president's cabinet. The president represents the United States around the world. He or she oversees relations with other countries and signs treaties. The president signs bills into law and appoints officials and federal judges. He or she also leads the military and manages government workers.

★ LEGISLATIVE BRANCH

The legislative branch makes laws, maintains the military, and regulates trade. It also has the power to declare war. This branch consists of the Senate and the House of Representatives. Together, these two houses make up Congress. Each state has two senators. A state's population determines the number of representatives it has.

★ JUDICIAL BRANCH

The judicial branch interprets laws. It consists of district courts, courts of appeals, and the Supreme Court. District courts try cases. If a person disagrees with a trial's outcome, he or she may appeal. If a court of appeals supports the ruling, a person may appeal to the Supreme Court. The Supreme Court also makes sure that laws follow the US Constitution.

THE PRESIDENT ★

★ QUALIFICATIONS FOR OFFICE

To be president, a person must meet three requirements. A candidate must be at least 35 years old and a natural-born US citizen. He or she must also have lived in the United States for at least 14 years.

★ ELECTORAL COLLEGE

The US presidential election is an indirect election. Voters from each state choose electors to represent them in the Electoral College. The number of electors from each state is based on the state's population. Each elector has one electoral vote. Electors are pledged to cast their vote for the candidate who receives the highest number of popular votes in their state. A candidate must receive the majority of Electoral College votes to win.

★ TERM OF OFFICE

Each president may be elected to two four-year terms. Sometimes, a president may only be elected once. This happens if he or she served more than two years of the previous president's term.

The presidential election is held on the Tuesday after the first Monday in November. The president is sworn in on January 20 of the following year. At that time, he or she takes the oath of office:

I do solemnly swear (or affirm) that I will faithfully execute the office of President of the United States, and will to the best of my ability, preserve, protect and defend the Constitution of the United States.

LINE OF SUCCESSION

The Presidential Succession Act of 1947 defines who becomes president if the president cannot serve. The vice president is first in the line of succession. Next are the Speaker of the House and the President Pro Tempore of the Senate. If none of these individuals is able to serve, the office falls to the president's cabinet members. They would take office in the order in which each department was created:

Secretary of State

Secretary of the Treasury

Secretary of Defense

Attorney General

Secretary of the Interior

Secretary of Agriculture

Secretary of Commerce

Secretary of Labor

Secretary of Health and Human Services

Secretary of Housing and Urban Development

Secretary of Transportation

Secretary of Energy

Secretary of Education

Secretary of Veterans Affairs

Secretary of Homeland Security

While in office, the president receives a salary of $400,000 each year. He or she lives in the White House and has 24-hour Secret Service protection.

The president may travel on a Boeing 747 jet called Air Force One. The airplane can accommodate 76 passengers. It has kitchens, a dining room, sleeping areas, and a conference room. It also has fully equipped offices with the latest communications systems. Air Force One can fly halfway around the world before needing to refuel. It can even refuel in flight!

Air Force One

If the president wishes to travel by car, he or she uses Cadillac One. It has been modified with heavy armor and communications systems. The president takes

— Cadillac One —

Cadillac One along when visiting other countries if secure transportation will be needed.

The president also travels on a helicopter called Marine One. Like the presidential car, Marine One accompanies the president when traveling abroad if necessary.

Sometimes, the president needs to get away and relax with family and friends. Camp David is the official presidential retreat. It is located in the cool, wooded mountains of Maryland. The US Navy maintains the retreat, and the US Marine Corps keeps it secure. The camp offers swimming, tennis, golf, and hiking.

When the president leaves office, he or she receives lifetime Secret Service protection. He or she also receives a yearly pension of $207,800 and funding for office space, supplies, and staff.

Marine One

George Washington

Abraham Lincoln

Theodore Roosevelt

	PRESIDENT	PARTY	TOOK OFFICE
1	George Washington	None	April 30, 1789
2	John Adams	Federalist	March 4, 1797
3	Thomas Jefferson	Democratic-Republican	March 4, 1801
4	James Madison	Democratic-Republican	March 4, 1809
5	James Monroe	Democratic-Republican	March 4, 1817
6	John Quincy Adams	Democratic-Republican	March 4, 1825
7	Andrew Jackson	Democrat	March 4, 1829
8	Martin Van Buren	Democrat	March 4, 1837
9	William H. Harrison	Whig	March 4, 1841
10	John Tyler	Whig	April 6, 1841
11	James K. Polk	Democrat	March 4, 1845
12	Zachary Taylor	Whig	March 5, 1849
13	Millard Fillmore	Whig	July 10, 1850
14	Franklin Pierce	Democrat	March 4, 1853
15	James Buchanan	Democrat	March 4, 1857
16	Abraham Lincoln	Republican	March 4, 1861
17	Andrew Johnson	Democrat	April 15, 1865
18	Ulysses S. Grant	Republican	March 4, 1869
19	Rutherford B. Hayes	Republican	March 3, 1877

THEIR TERMS ★

LEFT OFFICE	TERMS SERVED	VICE PRESIDENT
March 4, 1797	Two	John Adams
March 4, 1801	One	Thomas Jefferson
March 4, 1809	Two	Aaron Burr, George Clinton
March 4, 1817	Two	George Clinton, Elbridge Gerry
March 4, 1825	Two	Daniel D. Tompkins
March 4, 1829	One	John C. Calhoun
March 4, 1837	Two	John C. Calhoun, Martin Van Buren
March 4, 1841	One	Richard M. Johnson
April 4, 1841	Died During First Term	John Tyler
March 4, 1845	Completed Harrison's Term	Office Vacant
March 4, 1849	One	George M. Dallas
July 9, 1850	Died During First Term	Millard Fillmore
March 4, 1853	Completed Taylor's Term	Office Vacant
March 4, 1857	One	William R.D. King
March 4, 1861	One	John C. Breckinridge
April 15, 1865	Served One Term, Died During Second Term	Hannibal Hamlin, Andrew Johnson
March 4, 1869	Completed Lincoln's Second Term	Office Vacant
March 4, 1877	Two	Schuyler Colfax, Henry Wilson
March 4, 1881	One	William A. Wheeler

Franklin D. Roosevelt

John F. Kennedy

Ronald Reagan

	PRESIDENT	PARTY	TOOK OFFICE
20	James A. Garfield	Republican	March 4, 1881
21	Chester Arthur	Republican	September 20, 1881
22	Grover Cleveland	Democrat	March 4, 1885
23	Benjamin Harrison	Republican	March 4, 1889
24	Grover Cleveland	Democrat	March 4, 1893
25	William McKinley	Republican	March 4, 1897
26	Theodore Roosevelt	Republican	September 14, 1901
27	William Taft	Republican	March 4, 1909
28	Woodrow Wilson	Democrat	March 4, 1913
29	Warren G. Harding	Republican	March 4, 1921
30	Calvin Coolidge	Republican	August 3, 1923
31	Herbert Hoover	Republican	March 4, 1929
32	Franklin D. Roosevelt	Democrat	March 4, 1933
33	Harry S. Truman	Democrat	April 12, 1945
34	Dwight D. Eisenhower	Republican	January 20, 1953
35	John F. Kennedy	Democrat	January 20, 1961
36	Lyndon B. Johnson	Democrat	November 22, 1963

LEFT OFFICE	TERMS SERVED	VICE PRESIDENT
September 19, 1881	Died During First Term	Chester Arthur
March 4, 1885	Completed Garfield's Term	Office Vacant
March 4, 1889	One	Thomas A. Hendricks
March 4, 1893	One	Levi P. Morton
March 4, 1897	One	Adlai E. Stevenson
September 14, 1901	Served One Term, Died During Second Term	Garret A. Hobart, Theodore Roosevelt
March 4, 1909	Completed McKinley's Second Term, Served One Term	Office Vacant, Charles Fairbanks
March 4, 1913	One	James S. Sherman
March 4, 1921	Two	Thomas R. Marshall
August 2, 1923	Died During First Term	Calvin Coolidge
March 4, 1929	Completed Harding's Term, Served One Term	Office Vacant, Charles Dawes
March 4, 1933	One	Charles Curtis
April 12, 1945	Served Three Terms, Died During Fourth Term	John Nance Garner, Henry A. Wallace, Harry S. Truman
January 20, 1953	Completed Roosevelt's Fourth Term, Served One Term	Office Vacant, Alben Barkley
January 20, 1961	Two	Richard Nixon
November 22, 1963	Died During First Term	Lyndon B. Johnson
January 20, 1969	Completed Kennedy's Term, Served One Term	Office Vacant, Hubert H. Humphrey

	PRESIDENT	PARTY	TOOK OFFICE
37	Richard Nixon	Republican	January 20, 1969
38	Gerald Ford	Republican	August 9, 1974
39	Jimmy Carter	Democrat	January 20, 1977
40	Ronald Reagan	Republican	January 20, 1981
41	George H.W. Bush	Republican	January 20, 1989
42	Bill Clinton	Democrat	January 20, 1993
43	George W. Bush	Republican	January 20, 2001
44	Barack Obama	Democrat	January 20, 2009
45	Donald Trump	Republican	January 20, 2017
46	Joe Biden	Democrat	January 20, 2021

Barack Obama

★ PRESIDENTS MATH GAME ★

Have fun with this presidents math game! First, study the list above and memorize each president's name and number. Then, use math to figure out which president completes each equation below.

1. Joe Biden – Franklin Pierce = ?

2. Joe Biden – James Madison = ?

3. Joe Biden – Gerald Ford = ?

Answers: 1. Franklin D. Roosevelt (46 – 14 = 32)
2. Bill Clinton (46 – 4 = 42)
3. Martin Van Buren (46 – 38 = 8)

LEFT OFFICE	TERMS SERVED	VICE PRESIDENT
August 9, 1974	Completed First Term, Resigned During Second Term	Spiro T. Agnew, Gerald Ford
January 20, 1977	Completed Nixon's Second Term	Nelson A. Rockefeller
January 20, 1981	One	Walter Mondale
January 20, 1989	Two	George H.W. Bush
January 20, 1993	One	Dan Quayle
January 20, 2001	Two	Al Gore
January 20, 2009	Two	Dick Cheney
January 20, 2017	Two	Joe Biden
January 20, 2021	One	Mike Pence
		Kamala Harris

★ WRITE TO THE PRESIDENT ★

You may write to the president at:

The White House
1600 Pennsylvania Avenue NW
Washington, DC 20500

You may email the president at:

www.whitehouse.gov/contact

★ GLOSSARY ★

aneurysm—a bulge in a blood vessel.

cancer—any of a group of often deadly diseases characterized by an abnormal growth of cells that destroys healthy tissues and organs.

civil rights—rights that protect people from unequal treatment or discrimination.

Democrat—a member of the Democratic political party. Democrats believe in social change and strong government.

Democratic National Convention—a national meeting held every four years during which the Democratic Party chooses its candidates for president and vice president.

discrimination (dihs-krih-muh-NAY-shuhn)—unfair treatment based on factors such as a person's race, religion, or gender.

domestic violence—an act between members of a family or household that results in serious physical or emotional harm.

environment—all the surroundings that affect the growth and well-being of a living thing.

judiciary (joo-DIH-shee-ehr-ee)—the branch of a government in charge of courts and judges.

negotiate (nih-GOH-shee-ayt)—to work out an agreement about the terms of a contract.

pandemic—an occurrence in which a disease spreads very quickly and affects many people over a large area.

peninsula—land that sticks out into water and is connected to a larger landmass.

political science—the study of government and politics.

preparatory school—a typically private school that prepares students for college.

primary—a method of selecting candidates to run for public office. A political party holds an election among its own members to select the party members who will represent it in the coming general election.

racism—the belief that one race is better than another.

Republican—a member of the Republican political party. Republicans are conservative and believe in small government.

riot—a sometimes violent disturbance caused by a large group of people.

running mate—a candidate running for a lower-rank position on an election ticket, especially the candidate for vice president.

syllable—a word or part of a word pronounced as a unit with one sound.

tuition (tuh-WIH-shuhn)—money students pay to attend a school.

Vietnam War—from 1954 to 1975. A long, failed attempt by the United States to stop North Vietnam from taking over South Vietnam.

ONLINE RESOURCES

Booklinks
NONFICTION NETWORK
FREE! ONLINE NONFICTION RESOURCES

To learn more about Joe Biden, please visit **abdobooklinks.com** or scan this QR code. These links are routinely monitored and updated to provide the most current information available.

★ INDEX ★

A

Afghanistan, 4, 24

Archmere Academy, 12, 13

B

Balkan Peninsula, 20

Biden Cancer Initiative, 26

Biden Foundation, 26

Boggs, James Caleb, 14

C

California, 29

Capitol Building, US, 16

childhood, 10, 12, 13

China, 29

Clinton, Hillary, 22

Connecticut, 25

COVID-19 pandemic, 30, 32

D

Delaware, 10, 12, 13, 14, 15, 16, 17

Delaware, University of, 13

Democratic National Convention, 28, 29

Democratic Party, 14, 19, 22, 24, 28, 29

E

education, 12, 13

Europe, 20

F

family, 10, 12, 13, 14, 16, 17, 18, 19, 26

Floyd, George, 30

H

Harris, Kamala, 28, 29, 32

health, 19

I

Iraq, 4, 24

M

McCain, John, 22

McConnell, Mitch, 24

Minnesota, 30

N

New Castle County Council, 14

New START treaty, 24

New York, 13

North Atlantic Treaty Organization, 20

O

Obama, Barack, 4, 22, 24, 25, 26

P

Palin, Sarah, 22

Pennsylvania, 10

Presidential Medal of Freedom, 26

R

Republican Party, 14, 22, 24, 26

Russia, 24

S

Sanders, Bernie, 28

Sandy Hook Elementary School, 25

Senate, US, 4, 14, 15, 16, 17, 19, 20, 21, 24, 29

Senate Committee on the Judiciary, 20

Senate Foreign Relations Committee, 21

Soviet Union, 20

Syracuse University, 13

T

Trump, Donald, 26

V

Vietnam War, 15

Violence Against Women Act, 20

Violent Crime Control and Law Enforcement Act of 1994, 20

W

war, 4, 15, 20, 24

Warren, Elizabeth, 28

Washington, DC, 16, 17